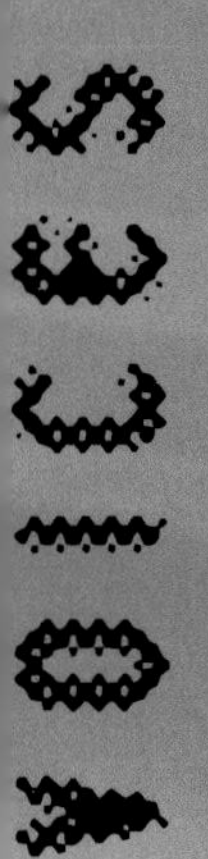

Violence

Cath Senker

Titles in the Voices series:

AIDS • Child Labour • Drugs on the Street • Gangs

Hunger • Poverty • Race Hate • Religious Extremism

Violence • Violence on the Screen • War

Published by Evans Brothers Limited
2A Portman Mansions
Chiltern Street
London W1U 6NR

VISIT OUR WEBSITE
Evans
www.evansbooks.co.uk

First published 2009

British Library Cataloguing in Publication Data
Senker, Cath
Violence. – (Voices)
1. Violence – Juvenile literature
I. Title
303.6

ISBN-13: 978 0 237 53721 0

Editor: Susie Brooks
Designer: Mayer Media Ltd
Picture research: Susie Brooks and Lynda Lines
Graphs and charts: Martin Darlison, Encompass Graphics

Produced for Evans Brothers Limited by
Monkey Puzzle Media Ltd
Little Manor Farm, The Street
Brundish, Woodbridge
Suffolk IP13 8BL, UK

Picture acknowledgements
Photographs were kindly supplied by the following: Alamy 11 (Photofusion Picture Library), 32 (Alex Segre), 36 (vario images GmbH & Co.KG); Corbis 25 (Angela Catlin), 28 (Ellen Ozier/Reuters); Getty Images 1 (Peter Scholey), 9, 12 (Dick Makin), 13 (Dennis Cox), 19, 20 (AFP), 21, 23 (Peter Scholey), 26 (Jeff Swensen), 39 (AFP), 45 (Jeff Swensen); PA Photos 16 (Cathal McNaughton/PA Archive); Panos 6–7 (GMB Akash), 8 (Moises Saman), 14 (Mikkel Ostergaard), 31 (Stuart Freedman), 33 (Justin Jin), 38 (Trygve Bolstad), 41 (Ian Teh), 42–43 (Justin Jin); Reuters front cover (Daniel Aguilar); Rex Features 15 (Burger/Phanie), 29 (Action Press), 35 (John Taylor), 37 (Chris Middlebrook); Topfoto.co.uk 24 (The Image Works), 30, 34 (ullstein bild), 40 (The Image Works).

Cover picture: Villagers in San Salvador Atenco, Mexico, clash with police who are attempting to evict a group of street vendors from the village.

The author would like to acknowledge the following sources: Action for Children, UK; Cheryl W., Silicon Valley Moms; Child Poverty Action Group, New Zealand; Auditi Guha, Somerville Journal, 'Youth speak up, talk about violence, drugs'; Tom Horvei, 'A Pacifist's View on Violence'; Sequella Thomas, 'Rap stereotypes not to blame for violent behavior'; Prof. Marian Tulloch, Sydney, Australia; UN, Our Right to be Protected from Violence, 2005; World Report on Violence against Children, 2006.

CONTENTS

WHAT IS VIOLENCE?

Violence is when someone uses force to hurt another person. It includes pushing and hitting people, and using weapons such as knives or guns. Violence can occur between individuals or between entire countries in a war.

Hurting people

Using words to bully people and hurt their feelings is a kind of violence. So is making them look small in front of other people. A boy in South Asia describes how it feels to be attacked in different ways:

" My father tied me to a tree and beat me in front of everyone in my neighbourhood because I was playing cards with my cousin. Now everyone in the neighbourhood teases me about it and this makes me feel worse than the actual beating. "

Distress shows on the face of this street child in Bangladesh, who has just had a fight with another boy.

"Violence takes place when someone uses their strength or their position of power to hurt someone else on purpose, not by accident. Violence includes threats of violence, and acts which could possibly cause harm, as well as those that actually do."

United Nations Secretary-General's 'Study on Violence against Children', 2006.

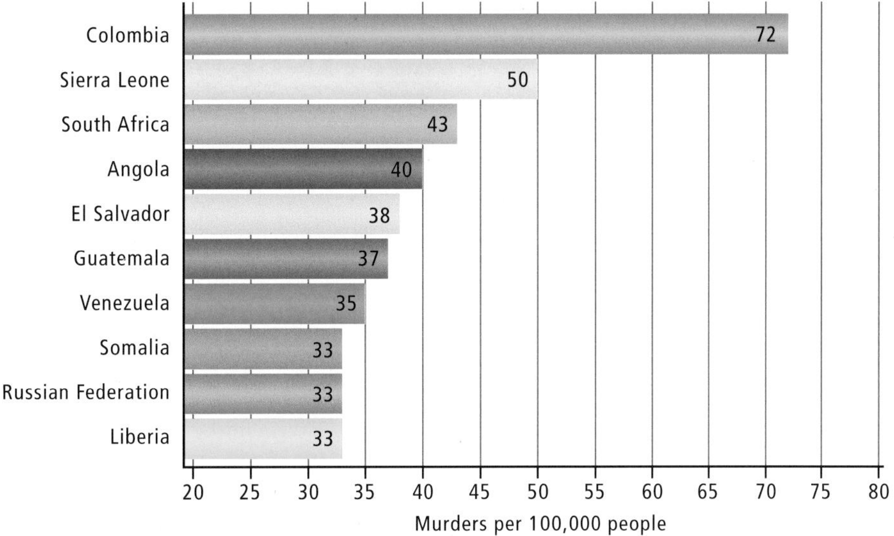

This graph shows the ten countries with the highest murder rates in 2004. These countries also have high levels of poverty.
World Health Organisation, 2004

Violent society

In the world's poorest countries, society itself is often violent. Many people are forced daily into long hours of backbreaking work. If they don't work, they go hungry. If they are injured, they cannot afford to see a doctor. They may be treated badly by people in positions of power. Ihab from Kenya thinks that poverty is a cause of violence:

" It seems to me that poverty can lead to violence. In poor African countries, resources like food are rare, so people fight over them. These struggles can even cause wars. "

"Poverty and general social disadvantage affect self-image – that can lead to substance dependency [drug addiction], spousal violence [abuse between husbands and wives] or mental health disorders, particularly depression."
'Poverty and Violence', a report by the Child Poverty Action Group, New Zealand.

ARE PEOPLE NATURALLY VIOLENT?

There has been violence throughout human history. People have fought wars, murdered their enemies and even used violence as entertainment. Is violence a part of human nature?

Making a killing

Some people believe that humans, like animals, have an instinct to use violence for survival. People have regularly fought or killed to gain power, land or precious resources from others. Sanan, 14, from Thailand, thinks that war is to be expected:

> **“All around the world, people kill each other in wars. I think people are naturally violent and that war is completely normal. War leads to change, and society needs change.”**

An armed Israeli soldier runs through the streets of Bethlehem, in the West Bank. There has been violent conflict between Israelis and Palestinians for decades.

These monks and nuns in Tibet pray for peace. Around the world, there are many religious and peace groups that work to solve conflict.

Keeping the peace

Many people feel that it is just as natural for human beings to co-operate. We work together to build towns and villages, to grow food and to trade. Around the world there are many peaceful societies that settle their arguments by talking. Many religious organisations promote peace, too. Takato, a 16-year-old from Japan, comments:

“ It's natural for people to be violent. But it's just as natural for them to be peaceful. We have large brains and we can work out how to live in peace if we set our minds to it. ”

"It is true that there is an infinite [unending] human capacity for violence. There is also an infinite potential for kindness. The unique ability of humans to *imagine* gives enormous power to idealism, an imagining of a better state of things not yet in existence."

Howard Zinn, *Declarations of Independence*, 1990.

ARE MEN MORE VIOLENT THAN WOMEN?

Throughout the world, it is mostly men who fight in armies and commit violent crime. Does this mean that men are naturally more violent than women?

Strong men

Men are commonly seen as stronger than women, and more aggressive. Traditionally, men were the ones who hunted animals and fought wars. Women cared for children and the home. Even though male and female roles have changed today, men and women still behave differently. Michael Thompson is a US expert on how boys grow up:

“ Mothers are always saying to me, ‘Why is my son racing around, not talking, and not listening? Why is he obsessed with playing war and shooting?’ ”

MEN AND MURDER

Most murderers in the USA are male, and most of the victims are male. In 2005:

- **Males were almost four times more likely than females to be murdered.**
- **Males were almost ten times more likely than females to carry out murder.**

US Bureau of Justice Statistics, 2005

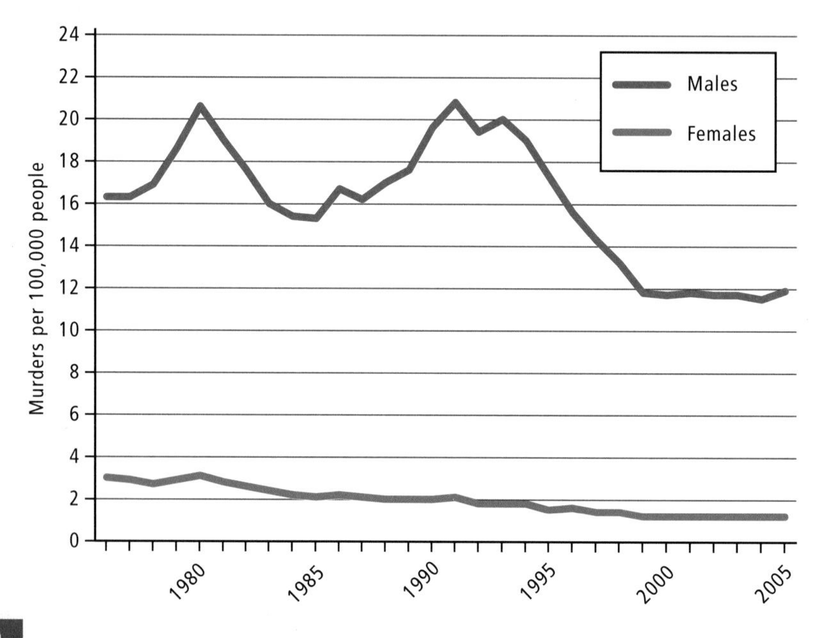

This graph compares the number of murders by men and by women in the USA over 30 years.
US Bureau of Justice Statistics, 2005

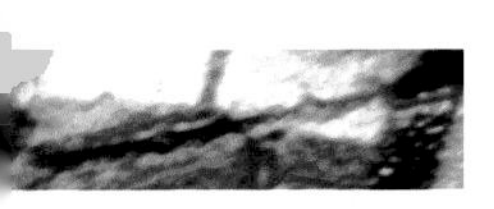

"[Girls are] just as aggressive as boys, though in a different way... [they] wage complicated battles with other girls, aimed at damaging relationships or reputations – leaving nasty messages by cellphone or spreading scurrilous rumours by e-mail."

Margaret Talbot of the New America Foundation, based on research by Kaj Bjorkqvist in Finland.

Members of a teenage girl gang bully another girl. Girls often hurt others by teasing or ignoring them. They may also pull their hair, push or hit them.

Aggressive girls

Some people argue that women can be just as violent as men. It depends on the situation. In Central America, for example, there are female gangs in poor areas that use knives and guns. Girl members become involved in violence and may even fight to the death. Zara joined a gang in Honduras:

" I thought joining a gang would be fun – I would have a group of mates. But they hit me and ordered me to do terrible things. They told me to rob people on the streets and then kill a girl from a rival gang. And I did it. "

WHY DOES DOMESTIC VIOLENCE HAPPEN?

Much of the violence in society goes on behind closed doors, between family members. Parents may abuse each other or their children. Why do some people turn against those they love?

A cycle of violence

Some people grow up in families with little money and poor housing. Stressed parents may become angry and lash out at other family members. Does this cause their children to behave violently as adults? Fatima, a teenager from France, believes there is a link:

"I'm not saying this happens to everyone, but if you are abused as a child, you will probably grow up an angry person. Because you had no control over your life when you were little, you may try to control others when you grow up. You have a higher risk than other people of becoming an abuser yourself."

A woman tries to protect herself from a violent partner. People may be angry because of problems in their lives and take it out on those who are closest to them.

This young girl has been hit by a parent or carer. Victims of child abuse often need special treatment to help them to get over their suffering.

Escaping the cycle

Not every abused child grows up to be a violent adult. And not all violent adults were abused when they were young. Some people believe that experiencing violence as a child makes people less likely to commit the same crime themselves. Giuseppina, 18, from Italy explains:

"People who put up with domestic violence as kids are often terrified they will become abusers themselves. They may seek help to deal with their anger and fears so that they don't become violent in the future."

VIOLENCE IN THE HOME

According to the United Nations (UN):

- **Around the world, one in three women has been beaten, forced to have sex or harmed in some other way.**
- **In New Zealand, Switzerland and the USA, between half and three-quarters of murders of children under ten are by one or both of the child's parents.**

United Nations Population Fund and World Report on Violence against Children, 2006

IS SMACKING CHILDREN ACCEPTABLE?

Parents smacking or hitting their children is the most common form of violence in families. Is this a sensible way to teach children to behave, or is it harmful?

Hitting home

Some parents feel that moderate violence, such as a smack, can be useful to discipline small children. For example, it teaches them to keep away from danger. People like Marsha, a UK mother of two, believe that smacking does not cause lasting damage. She says:

"I agree with smacking if it is used occasionally, for example, to stop dangerous behaviour. If a mum smacks her child in panic to stop him running out in front of a car, that's perfectly reasonable."

A Cambodian mother disciplines her son. Some people believe that the shock of a light smack reminds children not to misbehave again.

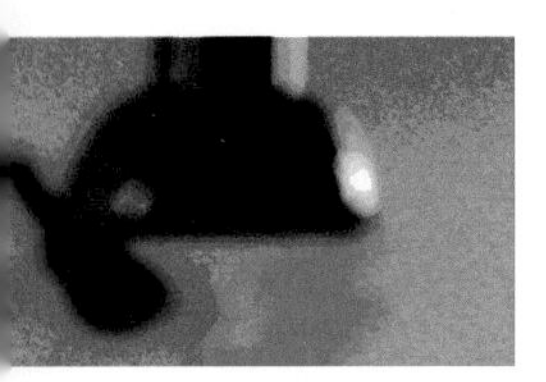

Missing the point

Others argue that children who are smacked learn to see violence as an acceptable form of punishment. For these people, violence does not teach children good behaviour – nor does it help them to understand why they are being punished. This was the experience of a youth leader in North America:

“ I remember being a foster child on another reserve [Native American living area]. I had been strapped... I never understood the reasons why or what I had done wrong... I do remember the fear and pain. ”

SMACKING DOESN'T WORK

According to a 2001 UNICEF survey in Europe and Central Asia, more than 75% of children said that hitting was never a good solution to problems at home.

This girl is behaving badly at school. Rather than punishing her, the teacher explains why her behaviour is dangerous.

“Young children frequently do not remember why they are hit, and children will only refrain from [stop] the misbehaviour if they face an imminent threat of being hit. This sort of punishment frightens children into certain behaviours: it does not help children to want to behave.”

‘Ending Physical and Humiliating Punishment of Children’, International Save the Children Alliance, 2005.

CAN RACIST VIOLENCE BE STOPPED?

Racism means treating others badly because they belong to a different race. People may be picked on for their skin colour, for example. Racist attacks range from bullying to brutal murder. Will racist violence ever end?

Fear of others

Some people think that it is natural to be suspicious of others who come from another background or have different customs. If they feel under threat, they may turn violently against the other group. Tano, 17, from Ghana, has little hope that this will change:

“ I know this sounds depressing but I don't think there's anything we can do to stop racism. There will always be bigoted people who can't understand others' point of view. As long as those people have power in the world, there will always be racism. ”

Family and friends mourn at the funeral of Nigerian teenager Christopher Alaneme. He was stabbed to death in a racist attack in the UK.

Stand up to racism

Other people argue that human beings are not born racist – they learn racist behaviour from others. Can people learn to be anti-racist too? Laila, a 16-year-old Lebanese girl in Australia, believes that education is the key:

" We should discuss the problems of racism more openly at school. Also, we should learn about other cultures as part of the curriculum. Then native-born Australians might realise that people from other countries have something to offer. If these things were discussed, maybe some of the racists at school would change their opinions. "

This bar chart shows the percentage rise or fall in racist crimes in European countries between 2000 and 2006. Although there was a huge rise in Denmark, the total figure was relatively low.
European Union Agency for Fundamental Rights, 2008

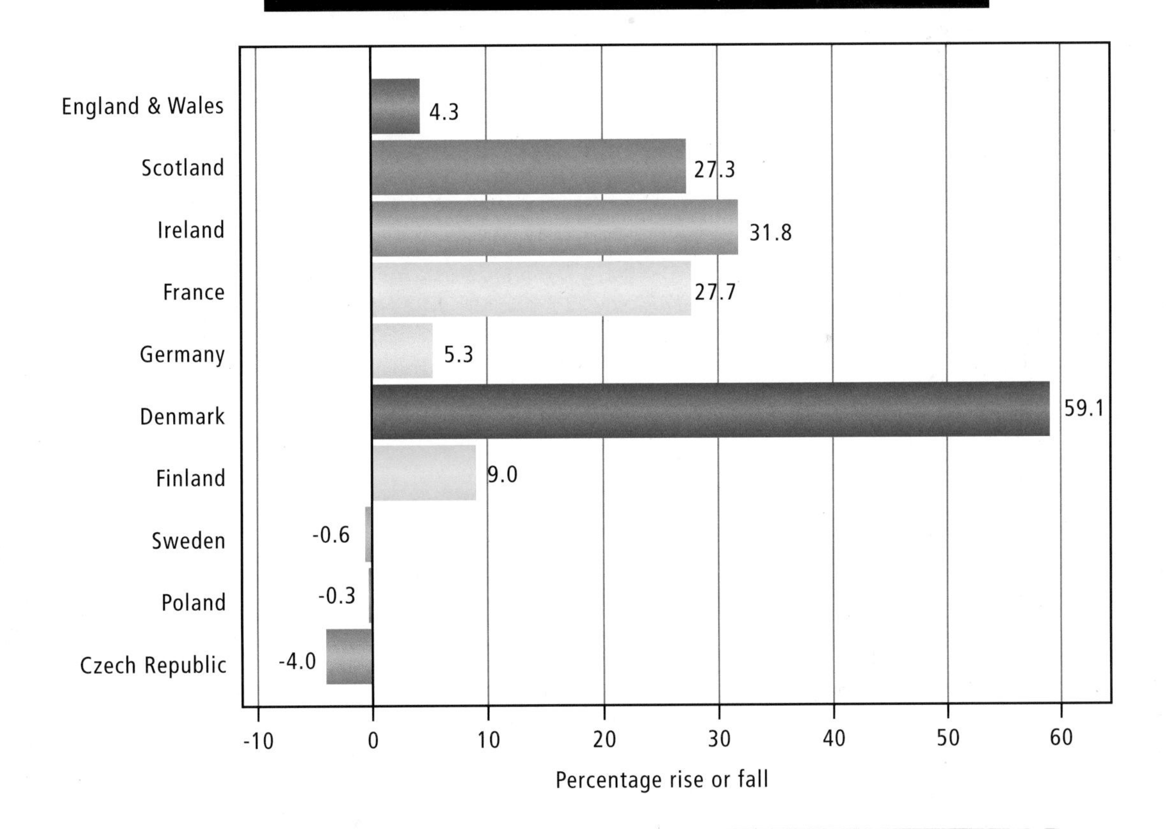

"No one is born hating another person because of the colour of his skin, or his background, or his religion. People must learn to hate, and if they can learn to hate, they can be taught to love."
Nelson Mandela, former president of South Africa, in his autobiography *Long Walk to Freedom.*

IS VIOLENT CRIME ON THE INCREASE?

Violent crime includes murder, assault and rape. Today's news reports are filled with examples of these terrible attacks. Is violent crime getting worse?

Guns and knives

Research shows that since World War II, there has been a gradual rise in violent crime. In many countries around the world, there are large numbers of dangerous weapons available. People seem more willing to use guns and knives to carry out crime or settle arguments. A young North American boy describes how fights can quickly flare out of control:

"Two kids were fighting and one of them pulled out a gun... because there were too many people around them he didn't do anything, but I think he would have taken a shot had there been no one around."

This graph shows the changing rate of recorded violent crime in four countries. There is a steep rise in England and Wales, mainly because there have been changes in the way crime is recorded.
Australian Institute of Criminology, 2006

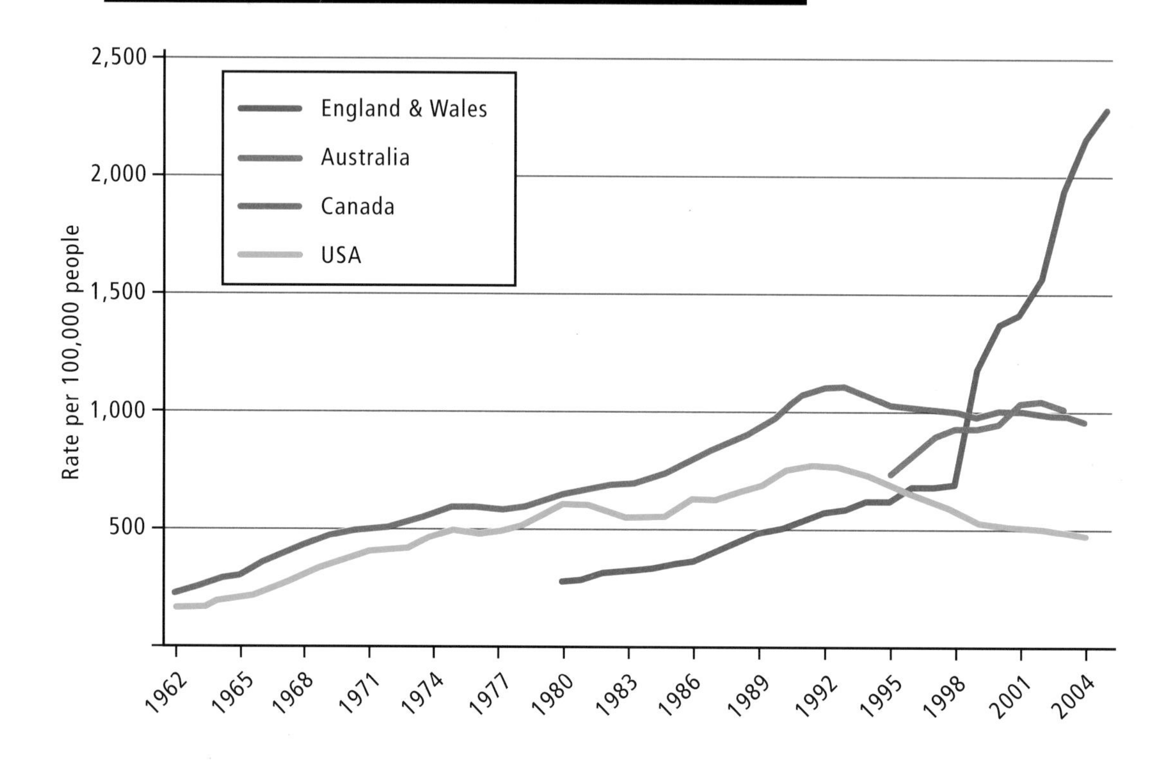

UK police officers stop a man to find out if he is carrying a knife. The police have become more cautious as more knife crimes are being reported.

More reports, not more crime

Some experts state that violence is not on the rise – there are just more people reporting violent crimes to the police. We are also made more aware of extreme cases, such as murders, because the media makes them headline news. A teenager in Brighton, UK feels that people have become over-suspicious:

“ Nowadays, everyone is afraid of guns and knives. The other day, there was a gang of kids causing trouble outside a bus, and the driver wouldn’t open the door for me to get on because he was afraid of knives or something similar. ”

IS ALCOHOL TO BLAME FOR VIOLENCE?

People who have drunk a large amount of alcohol are more likely to lose control in an argument. Does this mean that drinking alcohol causes violence?

Young people gather for an evening of drinking at a *botellon* in Valencia, Spain.

Sensible drinking

It is often argued that alcohol is not a problem if people drink sensibly. In many European countries, such as Italy and France, it is normal to enjoy beer or wine with a meal but not to get drunk. In Spain, many young people drink alcohol at outdoor street parties called *botellones*. These events rarely lead to violence, as 18-year-old Blanca from Seville explains:

" I sometimes do *botellon.* It's a brilliant way of hanging out with your friends without spending a fortune to get into a club. I don't drink that much anyway. Everyone has a laugh and I've never seen anyone turn violent. "

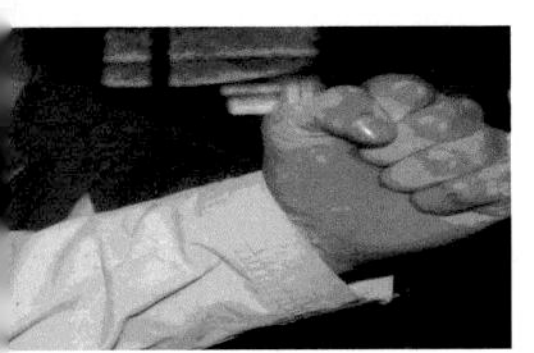

Binge drinking

People who are concerned about alcohol point to the rise in binge drinking among young people. This can lead to violence on the streets and anti-social behaviour, such as vandalism. Willem, 14, from Belgium thinks that teenagers should avoid alcohol:

“ Some teenagers think that it's cool to drink but they don't understand the dangers of alcohol. Someone at my school got so drunk he was arrested. Drinking is really stupid. ”

ALCOHOL ATTACKS

- **In Russia, 75% of people arrested for murder had drunk alcohol before the incident.**
- **In England and Wales, 50% of victims of interpersonal violence reported that their attacker had been drinking alcohol.**

'Interpersonal Violence and Alcohol', World Health Organisation, 2006

A binge drinker raises his fists on a night out in Glasgow, Scotland. For people who have drunk a lot of alcohol, light-hearted fights can quickly turn nasty.

"Throughout Scotland, communities report that youths under the influence of alcohol are blighting their communities through violence, vandalism and anti-social behaviour."

Assistant Chief Constable Neil Richardson, Scotland, 2006.

DO DRUGS MAKE PEOPLE VIOLENT?

Drug users may use violence to steal money to spend on drugs. They may become violent when they've taken drugs. Does taking drugs lead to violence or are there other issues involved?

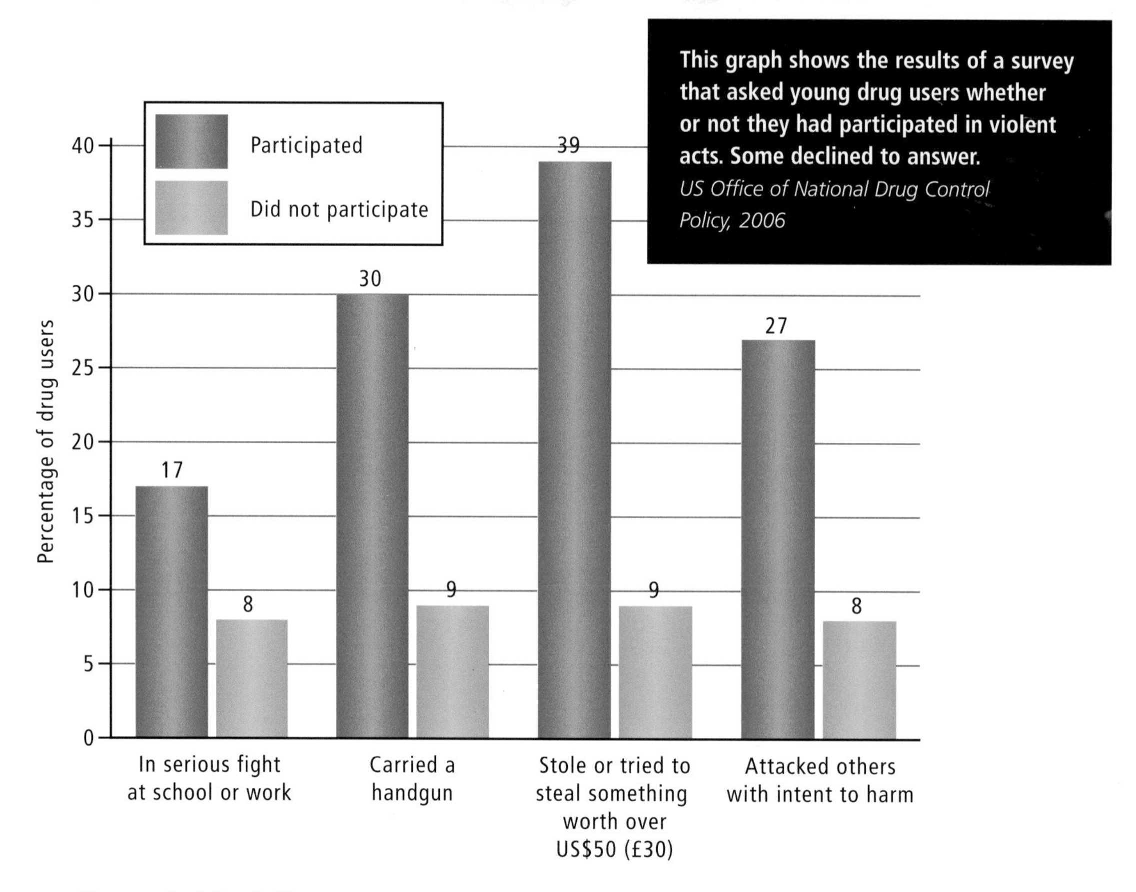

This graph shows the results of a survey that asked young drug users whether or not they had participated in violent acts. Some declined to answer.
US Office of National Drug Control Policy, 2006

Harmful habit

Some crime experts explain that when people have taken drugs, they cannot think clearly. This may lead them to carry out violent acts that they would not commit otherwise. Many people point to the violent behaviour of users who are desperate to get drugs, or traffickers who are involved in illegal drug sales. Carla was part of a drugs gang in Mexico:

" In my neighbourhood, it was normal to take drugs. It was normal to have guns, too. We bought them illegally and used them in armed robberies. We stole money at gunpoint to pay for our drugs. "

DRUGS V ALCOHOL

According to a Swedish survey:

- **10% of all violent crimes were carried out by people who had misused drugs.**
- **16% of all violent crimes were committed by people who had been in hospital for alcohol misuse.**

Researchers Martin Grann and Seena Fazel, 2003

Not a cause

Other experts believe it is unlikely that drugs make people violent. They say that violent criminals have other problems in their lives – they may even take drugs to try to forget about violent experiences. Some people argue that certain drugs make users more peaceful rather than more violent. Rachid from Denmark says:

“ Lots of people take drugs such as marijuana and ecstasy to chill out or lift their mood. I'm not saying it's right to take drugs, but these particular ones don't cause violence. ”

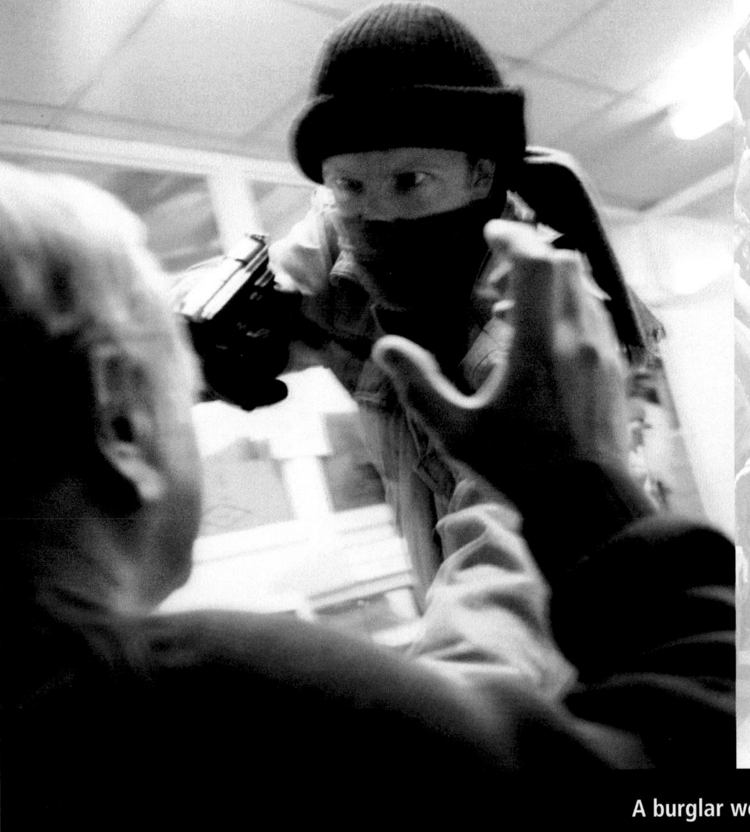

"It is usually the case that those committing violent acts under the influence of drugs have pre-drug use violent histories. Drugs can thus be a catalyst [something that prompts an action] in some cases but not a cause."

DrugScope, UK, 2008.

A burglar wearing a mask points a gun at a man. Many armed robberies are linked to drug use, but a significant number are not.

ARE GANGS ALWAYS VIOLENT?

Gangs are groups of young people who wear similar clothes, use the same symbols and spend time together. Gangs are blamed for much of the violence in inner cities. Is this fair?

A group of young people hang out on the street in Japan. There are criminal gangs in Japan called the *Yakuza*, but some gangs are simply groups of friends.

A group of mates

Not all gangs are seen as violent. Many teenagers join gangs because they share interests and hobbies or to avoid being bullied by members of other groups. Mira, 15, from Scotland says:

" Most people think gangs are all linked to drugs, alcohol and violence. But they're not all evil. Some of the gangs I know are just groups of friends who spend time together and stick up for each other. "

GANG CRIME

One survey of gangs in Central America showed that gangs are a major cause of criminal violence, responsible for somewhere between 10% and 60% of the total of violent crimes.

Envío Digital, December 2007

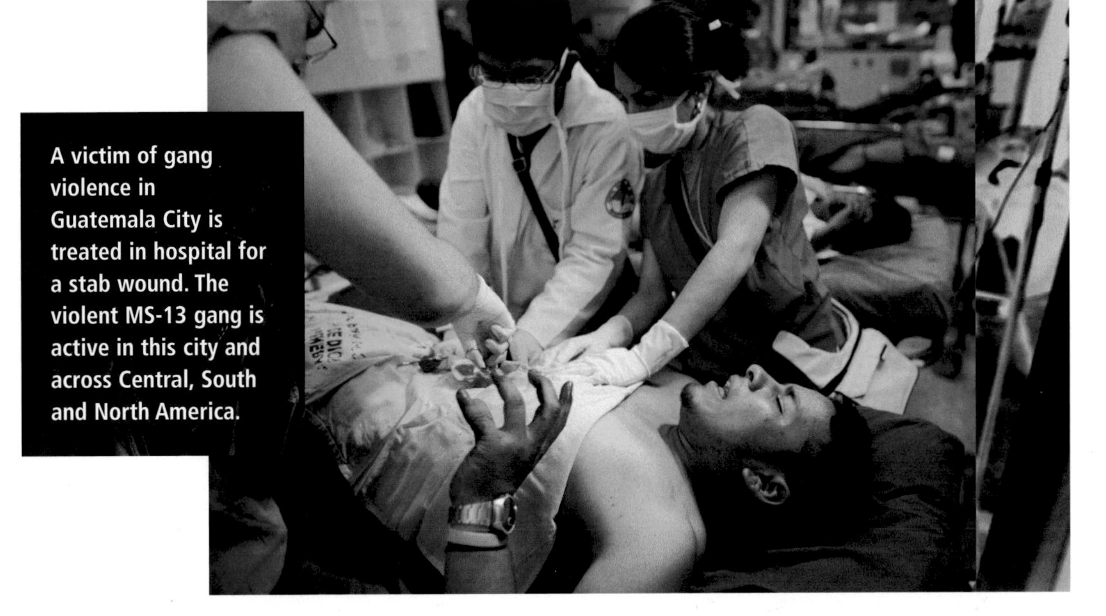

A victim of gang violence in Guatemala City is treated in hospital for a stab wound. The violent MS-13 gang is active in this city and across Central, South and North America.

A violent culture

Some experts argue that gangs are different from other youth groups. To them, violence is part of gang culture. Gang members often become victims of violence themselves. They also hurt innocent people. High-school student Terrell from Massachusetts, USA was shot by a gang although he was not a member. He now has to use a wheelchair:

“ After I was shot, I was in the hospital for two years. During that time, I lost four friends to shootings. I have seen what the streets can do, and what it has shown me is that no one is invincible. ”

“All gangs are violent or potentially [likely to become] violent. When young males come together as a gang, the group enables them to commit acts of violence and other anti-social behaviour that the individual members would not likely commit on their own.”

US researcher Dr Deborah Prothrow-Stith, *Deadly Consequences*, 1991.

SHOULD GUNS BE BANNED?

In some countries, including South Africa, the USA and several Latin American states, many people own a gun. Guns are used by the police, by criminals and by individuals against their enemies. Should they be allowed?

Guns protect you

In the United States, adults are allowed to own a gun to defend their homes. Some believe that when law-abiding people have guns, crime is reduced. In places where guns are forbidden, criminals will use them anyway. Naledi, 16, from South Africa, doesn't think that banning guns will stop violence in his country:

“ How do you think that banning guns will get rid of them? It's ridiculous! Criminals will ignore the law, so it'll just mean that they have guns and honest people don't. The bad guys won't stop killing people just because it's illegal! ”

This young woman in Pennsylvania, USA has just bought herself a gun for protection. Many Americans believe that owning a gun is their right as well as a part of their culture.

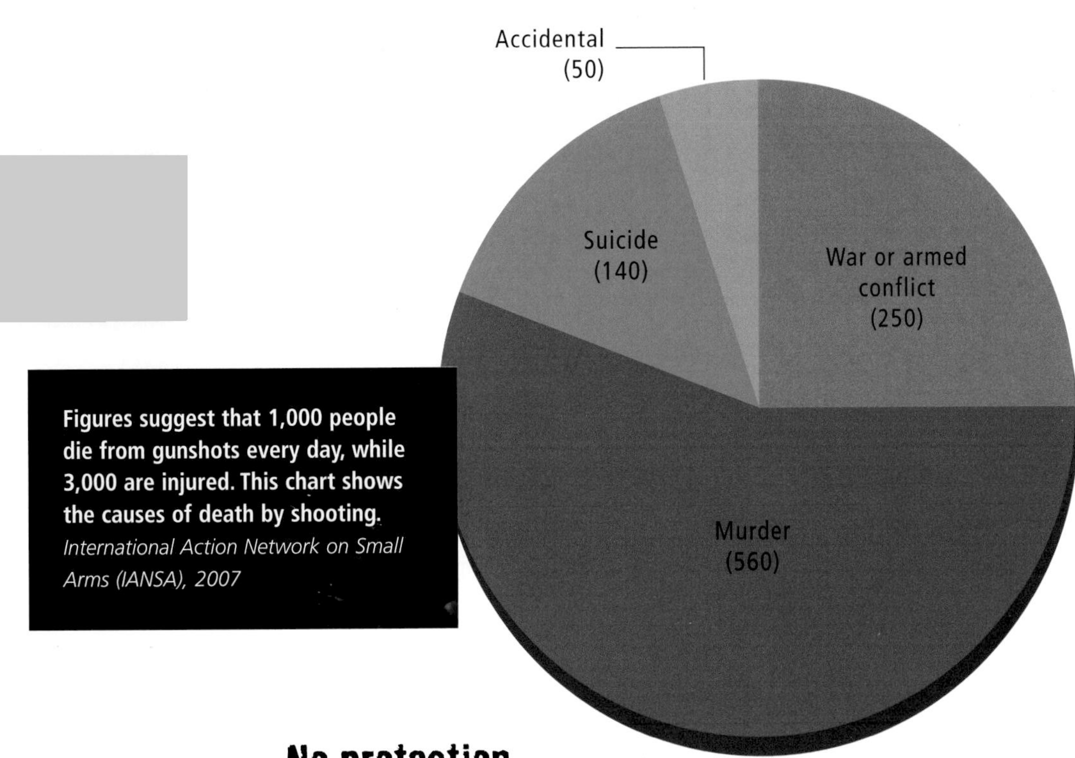

Figures suggest that 1,000 people die from gunshots every day, while 3,000 are injured. This chart shows the causes of death by shooting.
International Action Network on Small Arms (IANSA), 2007

No protection

Anti-gun campaigners reason that guns make society more violent. They are used in school shootings, domestic violence and robberies. When guns go off by accident, children are often the victims. Cheryl, from the USA, thinks it is nonsense to argue that guns protect people:

“The argument against guns is to SAVE LIVES! You do the maths. Personally, I've never heard of anyone using their gun to 'protect' themselves. Have you? When was the last time you heard a story in the news about a break-in where someone actually put a gun to good use?”

DANGEROUS WEAPONS

According to the International Action Network on Small Arms (IANSA):

- **74% of all guns are owned by civilians (including security guards), rather than police or the armed forces.**
- **A gun attack is 12 times more likely to kill than any other type of assault.**
- **A US study in 2003 showed that owning a gun increased the chances of death in the household, through murder, suicide or accident, by 41%.**

IANSA, 2007

IS VIOLENCE IN SPORT ACCEPTABLE?

Violent incidents often occur in competitive team sports. There are fist fights during ice hockey matches and deliberate fouls in football. Are these kinds of violence acceptable?

Violence is normal

Many researchers say that releasing pent-up aggression is a natural part of sport. All matches have referees who make sure no one gets badly hurt. Some people even think that violence makes sports more exciting. These 16-year-old boys in Sydney, Australia can't see any problem with a competitive brawl:

" I must admit a good punch up is good to see when the games are a bit boring... People who criticise are wimps and do-gooders... If they don't like the violence, they can turn it off. "

A Canadian ice-hockey player punches a member of the opposing team during a match. In 2008, strict penalties were introduced in Canada to try to stop violence on the ice.

"[In Canadian ice hockey] boys and young men are introduced to highly aggressive behaviour. In this and in many other sports subcultures, brutal body contact and physical assault are part and parcel of what it means to be a man."

Joseph Maguire, professor of the sociology of sport, Loughborough University, UK, 2006.

Russian football fans run riot in Moscow after their team was defeated in a World Cup game. Violent clashes between gangs of Russian football fans happen regularly.

Violence is wrong

Other people argue that it is possible to be competitive without being violent. They believe that violence in sport should be banned – after all, it is breaking the rules. Some spectators may pick up violent habits by watching aggressive games. Sam, 17, from Canada, believes in sensible play:

“ Violence in sports sets a bad example for the fans – especially kids. They'll see their favourite player fighting or insulting other players and think that violence and disrespect are perfectly acceptable. ”

IS SCREEN VIOLENCE DANGEROUS?

We see violence on the screens of TV, films, computer games and the Internet. It includes both fiction and real-life events on the news and in documentaries. Can screen violence cause people harm?

TV IN THE USA

According to the American Psychiatric Association, by the age of 18 an American will have seen 200,000 acts of violence and 16,000 murders on the screen.

Violent solutions

Film and game heroes often use violence to solve problems. Some viewers may interpret this as being acceptable in real life too. Many studies have shown that people who watch violent programmes become more aggressive. In a survey exploring violence against children in Europe and Asia, one young person said:

> **"The worst impact of TV violence is affecting children. They don't understand that what they see is wrong and that it's not something to follow. Instead, they understand that through violence we may resolve many things."**

The Batman action film, *The Dark Knight* contains scenes of intense violence. Many people were shocked that it was passed as suitable for children.

TV is not to blame

Other studies show that while many people watch screen violence, only a tiny minority attack in real life. This suggests that perhaps society is to blame, not the screen. If people see fighting at home or on the streets, they are more likely to regard it as normal. Dhara, from India, thinks the real world is the problem:

“ Sadly, the world is not just made up of nice people. It's easy just to blame the TV but actually there are bad people out there in real life. Children are just as likely to copy what they see on the streets as what they see on TV. ”

An Indian boy, living rough in New Delhi, points a toy gun. People may accept violence if they live in a violent area – whether or not they watch TV.

DO COMPUTER GAMES CAUSE AGGRESSION?

Many computer games simulate violence. To win the game, players often take actions to shoot and kill, spraying blood everywhere. Do these games encourage real-life violence?

Copycat violence

Some experts believe that game players are influenced by what they see. Young people can find it hard to separate the game from the real world. They may copy the violent acts as a way of dealing with their own challenges. One young American man was so addicted to violent games that it affected his life:

" I got hooked on *Grand Theft Auto 3* when I was a teenager. I couldn't stop playing – it was so exciting. When I grew up I joined the army to get some real action. "

A boy makes a 'virtual attack' in the violent computer game *Grand Theft Auto*. The game is not supposed to be played by children under 18.

Two boys fight in a school playground in Germany. There may be many reasons for this type of behaviour; experts fail to agree over whether screen violence is a cause.

AGGRESSIVE GAMES

A US survey showed that:

- **Boys who play 'teen'- or 'mature'-rated games for at least 40 minutes a day may see over 180 incidents of aggression per day.**
- **In 98% of the games, aggression goes unpunished.**

'Popular Video Games: Quantifying the Presentation of Violence and its Context' by S L Smith, K A Lachlan and R Tamborini, 2003

Stress buster

Other researchers insist that players do understand the difference between games and real life. According to them, gamers enjoy playing because it helps to relieve stress, but they rarely go on to attack others. Nicholas, a Russian teenager, believes that violent youngsters are driven by different issues:

" When people play computer games, they know it's not for real. It doesn't make them aggressive. People who turn violent usually had a bad childhood. "

"Instead of looking for a simple, direct relationship between video game violence and violent behavior in all children, we should be asking how we might identify those children who are at greatest risk of being influenced by these games."

US researchers, Dr Lawrence Kutner and Dr Cheryl Olson, *Grand Theft Childhood*, 2008.

DO RAPPERS MAKE VIOLENCE GLAMOROUS?

Rappers often sing about committing crime and using weapons. They look tough and pose for photos with guns. Do they make people think that violence is glamorous?

Telling the truth

Rap fans say that rappers tell the truth about their society. They often come from extremely poor areas with high levels of crime, drug use and violence. Just because people enjoy the music doesn't mean they'll go out and use a gun. Sequella, a student in Tennessee, USA, believes that rap is harmless:

" As a young girl I grew up around rap music that sang of violence, drugs, even sex. Like all the other children, I sang along with these rappers as well as the gospel music I listened to, but never did I do any of the actions that were promoted in the lyrics of the rap songs, because I was taught that those actions were wrong. "

Music fans often idolise the stars on stage, but do they act on what they hear? Many rap fans find it unfair that their choice of entertainment is criticised.

Not the whole truth

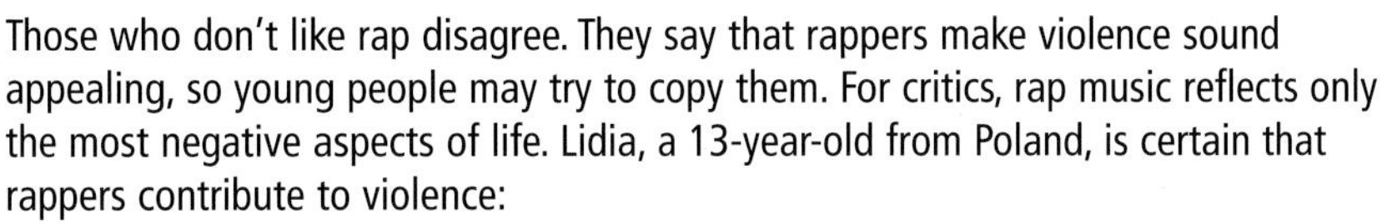

Those who don't like rap disagree. They say that rappers make violence sound appealing, so young people may try to copy them. For critics, rap music reflects only the most negative aspects of life. Lidia, a 13-year-old from Poland, is certain that rappers contribute to violence:

" Just listen to the lyrics! Rappers glorify street violence, gang warfare and gun culture. They're sexist towards women too, and encourage violence against them. "

The rapper 50 Cent performs at an award ceremony. Critics say that his raps about drugs, guns and crime glamorise violence and have a bad influence on young people.

"Researchers have found that exposure to violent or anti-social rap videos can increase aggressive thinking, but no research has yet tested how such exposure directly affects physical aggression."

National Youth Violence Prevention Resource Center, USA, 2008.

IS CENSORSHIP A GOOD MEANS OF PROTECTION?

Censorship is the attempt to stop people from accessing materials that are seen as inappropriate or harmful. For example, there is an age-rating system for films and games. Does censorship shield children from violence?

A useful tool

People who support censorship say that it helps parents and teachers to monitor what their children watch. They believe it is important to protect children from violence and other unsuitable material. Vera, an 18-year-old from Russia, agrees with censorship:

“When I go to the cinema, I want to be entertained, to escape from the ugliness of real life. Nowadays, you see sex, drugs and violence at the movies – which leads to a rise in crime. I believe all this filth should be banned from our screens.”

A customer looks through DVDs of horror films. Each one has an age rating and advice on whether the DVD contains violence, swearing or sexual content.

Better education

Those who are against censorship claim that it cannot solve the problem of violence in society. For them, it is more important to educate people so they learn to be sensible viewers and game players. Paul, a Canadian teen, believes that censorship can even hold people back:

" I agree that schools should block some websites that show harmful materials. But the trouble is that many of the sites we need to access for our schoolwork are censored too. It makes using the Internet really frustrating. "

Children need to learn how to use the Internet responsibly. School computers have filters that block certain websites, but these are not always reliable.

"Filters can't give kids critical thinking and good judgement. We have to teach them those skills. Students using a school computer that blocks access to hate sites, for example, won't get an opportunity to recognise that type of material or know how to discuss it when they see it."

Cathy Wing, Media Awareness Network, Canada, 2005.

IS IT EVER RIGHT TO FIGHT?

If someone attacks your friend, do you hit back or run away? People who are not normally violent may occasionally fight to defend themselves or others. Are they right to do so?

Peaceful solutions

Some people are pacifists. They say that violence breeds violence, and it is never right to fight or take a life. For a pacifist, even fighting back in self-defence is wrong. The belief that there is always a better way to solve problems is something that Tom, from Norway, understands:

“ Pacifism is not about not killing flies or just standing still watching while your family is attacked. Pacifism is about solving conflicts long before they ever come to a point where guns, rockets and cluster bombs are mentioned. ”

This knotted-gun sculpture in Malmo, Sweden is a symbol of anti-violence. Violent crime among young people is low in this Scandinavian country.

Lebanese children learn Taekwondo, a popular martial art. Taekwondo focuses on self-defence using controlled fighting techniques.

YOUNG FIGHTERS

A 2000–2001 World Health Organisation study looked at fighting among young people aged 11, 13 and 15 in 35 countries, mostly in Europe and North America. The rates varied greatly by country and region, but on average:

- **39% of those surveyed had been in at least one fight during the previous year.**
- **10% had been in three or more fights.**

Self-defence is no offence

People who are not pacifists argue that sometimes fighting back saves lives. It is not always possible to reason with an attacker. For example, if a bully grabs you and starts to choke you, you have to use force in return. Chizuko, from Japan, thinks that learning self-defence is vital:

“When I was at school, I was badly bullied by children much older than me. I used to come home in tears. My parents decided to send me to kickboxing classes. A few years later, I was attacked by a gang of girls in high school and at least I knew how to fend them off.”

IS THERE A WAY TO END VIOLENCE?

There is violence in every country in the world. It occurs within families, on the streets and in schools and workplaces. Wars break out between different regions and countries. Is it possible to create an entirely peaceful society?

Tough laws

Some people believe that governments need to have armed police, strong laws and harsh prison sentences to show that violence is not acceptable. If they crack down firmly on offenders, people are less likely to turn to violence. Lotte, 19, from the Netherlands, feels that prison is the only answer:

“ It's our right to be protected from violent criminals. Society will only be safe when these wrongdoers are all locked up. If there's a shortage of prisons, then build more. ”

PRISON IN THE USA

The USA locks up the highest number and percentage of its population: over 1 in 100 adults – more than 2.3 million people (2008).

Pew Center on the States, 2008

In some US states, courts can give a death sentence to people convicted for the most serious crimes, such as murder. This prisoner in Texas waits on death row for his sentence to be carried out.

"Governments cannot do it alone... Until we all answer the call through a greater emphasis on finding peaceful remedies to conflicts, deglamorising violence, and expanding opportunities, especially for youth, we will all remain hostage to violence."

Donna E Shahala, Secretary of Health and Human Services, California, USA.

This 18-year-old boy in Rio de Janeiro, Brazil traffics drugs for money to survive. In the slums, the average age to which a drug dealer can expect to live is just 23.

A fairer society

Others argue that violence will only be reduced through education and the creation of a fairer society. If everyone has schooling, a decent job, a home and enough to eat, people are less likely to feel the need to fight each other. Michael, 15, is from the USA, which imprisons a huge number of people:

" Sending people to prison clearly does not put them off committing further crimes. Just look at the statistics! Instead, the US government should work to prevent the causes of crime, for example, poverty. "

TIMELINE

27 BC–AD 476 Gladiator fights are a popular form of entertainment under the Roman Empire.

16th century The Hutterite pacifist community is formed in Austria and South Germany.

1790s The first street gangs appear in the USA.

1791 An amendment to the US Constitution allows people the right to 'keep and bear Arms'.

1960s The use of illegal drugs grows in Western nations.

1964 The US Civil Rights Act makes it illegal to treat people differently because of their race.

1968 In the USA, a voluntary film rating system is brought in to stop children from watching unsuitable films.

1970s In Western countries, people begin to see domestic violence as a crime rather than as a private matter in the home.

1970s Rap music becomes popular in the USA and spreads around the world.

Late 1970s The first games for personal computers are developed.

1980s Gangs of Central Americans form in the USA.

By late 1980s Street gangs in the USA with links to the drugs trade are common.

1989 The Children Act in the UK allows the police and local government to intervene in families to protect children at risk from violence.

1980s–1990s There is huge growth in male and female gangs in the USA.

1980s–1990s Rapid developments in computer technology in Western countries allow children increasing access to the media, such as videos. Ratings systems are developed to try to limit the amount of sex and violence that children see on screen.

1990 The US Crime Control Act makes it illegal to have a firearm at a school.

Early 1990s The general public gain access to the Internet.

1990s Computer-game designers use 3D graphics to make games look more realistic. The new games include first-person 'shooters' in which the game environment is seen from the player's view.

1993 The United Nations issues a Declaration on the Elimination of Violence Against Women.

1994 The USA passes the Violence Against Women Act to combat domestic violence.

1995 A US law states that all new TV sets bigger than 13 inches (33 cm) must have a V-chip fitted, which allows the user to stop certain programmes being shown – especially programmes containing sex or violence.

1997 The first *Grand Theft Auto* video game is published, a game with a high level of violence in which players fight criminals.

2000 A UK law allows the police to stop suspected football hooligans from travelling abroad for football matches.

Early 2000s Roughly 360 million people, or 6 per cent of the world's population, have access to the Internet.

2004–2005 UK laws make it illegal for parents to smack their children hard enough to leave a mark.

2006 Spain brings in a law that allows local councils to ban *botellones* – street drinking parties.

2006 The United Nations produces a study on violence against children and how to prevent it.

2007 It is reported that binge drinking is becoming more common in Mediterranean countries, such as Spain.

2008 There are roughly 1,500 million Internet users worldwide – about 22 per cent of the global population.

GLOSSARY

abuse To treat a person in a cruel or violent way, including sexually.

addicted Dependent on, or devoting so much time to something that it becomes difficult to give up.

aggressive Angry, and seeming likely to use violence.

anti-social behaviour Behaviour that is harmful or annoying to other people.

assault A physical attack on a person.

bigoted Having strong, unreasonable beliefs.

binge drinking Drinking a large amount of alcohol in a short space of time.

botellon (say: 'botayon') An outdoor party in Spain at which people drink alcohol and socialise.

civilian A person who is not a member of the armed forces or the police.

discipline Training people to follow rules and punishing them if they do not.

domestic violence Threatening behaviour or violence against another member of a household.

ecstasy An illegal drug that people take to give them energy; it can damage the body.

filter On a computer, a filter blocks websites that are not suitable for the user, for example, sites containing violence or sex.

foster child A child that is cared for over a period of time by a family that is not his or hers.

instinct An inborn characteristic or pattern of behaviour.

interpersonal Between two or more people.

marijuana An illegal drug that people take to help them relax; it can damage the body.

pacifist A person who believes that violence is always wrong.

racism Unfair treatment or violent behaviour towards people of a different race.

rape Forcing a person to have sex.

resources Goods, raw materials, money and services used by people to achieve a goal.

simulate To fake or imitate something so that it is very life-like.

subculture A group of people within society with their own behaviour and beliefs that are different from those of most people.

suicide The act of deliberately killing yourself.

trafficker Someone who buys and sells illegal drugs.

United Nations (UN) An international organisation with over 190 member countries, which was formed in 1945 to promote world peace, good health and economic development.

vandalism The crime of deliberately damaging property.

RESOURCES

Books

The Causes of School Violence by Helga Schier (Abdo Publishing Company, 2008)

Gangs (Voices) by Clive Gifford (Evans Brothers, 2006)

Gun Control by Mitchell Young (Greenhaven Press, 2006)

Violence in the Media by LeeAnne Gelletly (Lucent Books, 2004)

Violence in Society: The Impact on Our Lives by Ronda Armitage (Hodder Wayland, 2005)

Violence on the Screen (Voices) by Clive Gifford (Evans Brothers, 2006)

Websites

http://news.bbc.co.uk/cbbcnews/default.stm
The CBBC newsround site includes young people's contributions to several debates related to violence in society.

http://www.crimestoppers-uk.org/media-centre/case-studies
Case studies about children and adults involved with Crimestoppers in the UK.

http://www.gangsorus.com
A US site with information about many kinds of gangs.

http://www.idebate.org
The website of the International Debate Education Association, which includes Debatabase, a list of debating topics with arguments for and against.

http://www.unicef.org/violencestudy/childfriendly.html
A United Nations site with materials for young people about protecting children from violence.

INDEX